A Practical Guide for Improving Sales and Operations Planning

Supply Chain Consultants, Inc

5460 Fairmont Drive, Wilmington, DE 19808

Phone (302) 738-9215 • Fax (302) 454-7680

CONTRIBUTORS

Ed Mahler, Jane Lee and all the consultants at Supply Chain
who have worked tirelessly to make our clients successful.

Cover design by Cynthia Martinez

LIBRARY OF CONGRESS CATALOGING-IN-PUBLICATION DATA

Supply Chain Consultants -

A Practical Guide for Improving Sales and Operations Planning

ISBN-10: 0-9823148-0-9

ISBN-13: 978-0-9823148-0-7

Contents

PREAMBLE 1

Strategic Choice – Automate or Innovate 1

Improving Supply Chain Planning 4

Audience 5

Our Approach 5

THE CASE FOR SALES AND OPERATIONS PLANNING 8

What is S&OP? 8

Why Plan? 10

FIVE STEPS TO SUCCESS 13

Step 1: Understand Customer Demand 15

Step 2: Analyze Inventories 18

Step 3: Routinely Create a Demand Plan 20

Step 4: Balance Supply and Demand 24

Step 5: Implement Sales and Operations Planning (S&OP) 27

ORGANIZING SUPPLY CHAIN DATA 32

Identifying Data Attributes 32

Using Data for Forecasting 38

Adding Detail to an Aggregated Forecast 40

Using Data for Inventory Analysis 41

Analyzing Inventory Data 43

Identifying Aged Inventory 44

IMPROVING THE BUSINESS PROCESSES   **48**

Documenting the Current State   **48**

Designing the New Process   **51**

Extending Participation   **54**

Implementation Considerations   **58**

MODELING THE SUPPLY CHAIN   **60**

Methodology   **61**

Identifying Business Parameters   **63**

Example of a Planning Model for a Multi Site Manufacturing Company   **66**

Model Validation and Calibration   **70**

METRICS AND PERFORMANCE MEASUREMENT   **74**

You Cannot Improve What You Can't Measure   **74**

Causes, Concerns and Consequences   **76**

SUSTAINING SUPPLY CHAIN PLANNING IMPROVEMENTS   **86**

Why Do Companies Regress?   **87**

When Do Companies Sustain Improvements?   **88**

What Can Companies Do?   **89**

Preamble

Strategic Choice – Automate or Innovate

Most companies look at supply chain operations in one of two ways. They either regard the supply chain as a necessary evil to be managed efficiently and at minimal cost, or they regard the supply chain as central to their business.

The first category of companies has a financial view of their operations. For them, the primary purpose of the organization is to manage financial streams. In the minds of the managers, the company's success is not tied to delivering goods or services; rather, it is tied to utilizing funds and capital to generate profitable revenue streams.

An extreme example of this type of company was the dot com startup in the late 90's. The company used investor capital to create a buzz so that it could sell stock and accumulate capital funds. The capital funds were then used to fund operations. The view was that the stream of investor funds and capital funds would eventually be replaced by operating revenue – but that was not really critical as long as overall cash flow could be sustained. Ultimately, many of the startups did not offer value-adding products or services and the revenue streams collapsed.

The second category of companies has a business view that is primarily tied to the delivery of goods and services. For example, Toyota considers itself to be in the business of producing transportation vehicles profitably, and not primarily in the business of utilizing capital to make more money.

The different perspectives can obviously lead to starkly different strategic choices. If operations are primary, then profitability is tied to maintaining marketable goods and services. Hence there is a greater emphasis on product development and maintaining a portfolio of products that will sustain the business. Companies with a strong financial view are most concerned with exploiting the existing portfolio to generate immediate revenue.

The difference in perspectives also leads to how the supply chain and supply chain planning is viewed. The financial view of companies dictates that the supply chain should be simplified and automated to reduce costs. The operational view encourages using the supply chain as an integral portion of delivering goods and services. It regards the supply chain as a competitive differentiator and strives to make it as efficient as possible.

	Financial View	Operational View
Supply Chain Decision Processes	1. Automate decision processes. 2. Simplify decision making by creating functional islands that are highly automated. 3. Plan for certainty. Restrict judgment. 4. Provide minimal customer service. 5. Reduce costs.	1. Create competitive differentiators. 2. Exploit intrinsic strengths. 3. Integrate decision making to create a flexible and responsive supply chain. 4. Develop a robust framework for making decisions. 5. Plan for uncertainty

	Financial View	Operational View
Supply Chain Planning Technology	1. Leverage transaction systems and adopt standard procedures. 2. Limit planning horizon 3. Automate and enforce responses that are guided by strict rules.	1. Quantify decision making. 2. Deliver information to decision makers. 3. Provide tools to deal with market uncertainty.

A recent example may help to illustrate how the difference in perspectives can affect decision making. Company A had a robust supply chain planning program in place that had an integrated view of its manufacturing and logistics. Company B, on the other hand, had structured its supply chain to reduce costs. Its logistics was outsourced.

When fuel prices went up by 30 percent, Company A was able to re-optimize and use fewer trucks at the expense of more inter-modal and slightly higher inventory. As a result, its freight cost per pound only increased by an equivalent of 8% of the increase in fuel price. Company B absorbed the entire 30 percent fuel cost increase.

In the last ten years, the financial view has become prevalent. This has been encouraged by a triumvirate of technology vendors, consultants, and IT professionals. It is our view that this perspective is certainly relevant to a portion of all companies, but is not necessarily the universal long term sustainable solution. We believe that the financial view of operations is particularly useful for those companies with:

1. Relatively predictable demand. These companies don't have a need to react to market changes dynamically.

2. Cost structures in which manufacturing is not central. Such companies normally have a "product" or brand view and manufacturing is viewed as strictly a service provider. In general, these companies have low manufacturing costs compared to R&D and marketing.

Improving Supply Chain Planning

This book is intended for those companies that hold an operational view of their business. It is also a "How To" book. Our experience is that the biggest issue is not what needs to be done, but how to make improvements while keeping the day-to-day operations running. Time and again, we have seen mega improvement projects fail because they concentrate more on the end state and less on the process of getting to the end state. This book is an attempt to correct that.

The most efficient way for improving Supply Chain Operations Planning is to work on the business process and tools simultaneously. While it is theoretically possible to improve the process and supporting tools sequentially, it takes longer to get to the improved state because:

1. The process improvements need to be adjusted to the data that is available. Identifying process improvements in a vacuum often results in business process changes that cannot be supported by data quality and data availability.

2. Tools can only be developed if they are used and validated in practice. When the business processes are changed in conjunction with the tools, it provides a framework to check and validate the tools as they are put into use.

3. Developing tools and processes simultaneously allows the tool development to be guided by what is needed by the business, and not what is desirable from a theoretical perspective.

4. Developing a process without the tools to automate data collection and analysis slows down the adoption of the new processes.

The Sales and Operations Planning (S&OP) process is normally the core tactical planning process for a business. Our belief is that an effective S&OP process is the key to running an effective supply chain. An effective S&OP process provides the necessary framework for introducing initiatives like Six Sigma and lean manufacturing because the S&OP provides a framework to identify areas that need improvement.

We have laid out the supply chain improvement process as a series of logical steps that culminate in the implementation of an S&OP business process.

Each step of our implementation process is designed to provide value to the business, and is easy to digest. Taken together, the five steps provide a structured path for improving S&OP.

We do not expect that practitioners will be able to implement the entire improvement process described here from start to finish. Most businesses have elements of S&OP already in place. In this case, a business will have to implement small projects to fill in the gaps in the process or tools. A dedicated Supply Chain Manager should be able to extract enough useful information from this book to construct his/her own improvement program. However, we would still advocate using the five steps as a guide to audit the existing process.

For any improvement process, three key elements are required to succeed:

1. A well-defined focus at each step with measurable deliverables.

2. The will within the organization to drive integration across functions that often act as independent silos.

3. The right software tools.

Audience

This document is intended as:

1. A guide to the Supply Chain Manager leading the improvements.

2. An introduction for the project team members implementing Supply Chain Planning improvements.

3. An overview for the management of the business functions involved in the change process.

Our Approach

Although every house is different, the steps for building a house, the materials used, and the tools employed, are largely the same. The foundation is first, followed by the walls, and then the roof. It is technically possible to change this order, but with increased cost and a greater risk of failure.

Similarly, every company's supply chain decision making is unique, because every business is unique. The process of developing an effective S&OP process however, the software tools that support it, and the ending functionality are very similar. The most robust starting point is basic analysis of customers and products. This lays the foundation for creating a projection of future customer demand, which we call Demand Planning. This projection of future demand is a prerequisite for S&OP.

Next, to plan supply, a company needs a good picture of the starting point provided by inventory. This is combined with capacity limitations to come up with a quantitative representation (model) of the supply chain. A model provides the framework for analyzing different alternatives. Capacity restrictions need not be just manufacturing restrictions. Capacity restrictions may include raw material availability, transport capacity, warehouse capacity, and restrictions on other resources that can constrict the flow of material in a timely manner.

Once there is agreement on the underlying model, the company has to institute a disciplined process to use the model for routine planning.

We lay out this approach as five distinct steps:

1. Understand customer demand.

2. Analyze inventories.

3. Routinely create a demand plan.

4. Create a quantitative model to balance supply and demand.

5. Implement the Sales and Operations Planning process.

The same sequential approach is also effective when improving a process that is partially implemented. The goals, tasks, and deliverables outlined for each step can be used to audit the existing S&OP process and provide a framework for improvements.

In most cases, software tools are needed to support the S&OP process. The software approach that has proved to be successful stresses:

1. **Building on accumulated knowledge**. Tool development alternates with periods when the tools are actively used by the business. The knowledge gained guides the next cycle of tool development.

2. **Quick deliverables**. The overall effort is broken up into a series of six-to-eight week deliverables. In addition to being a project milestone, each deliverable provides concrete value to the business.

3. Application development is guided by a **high-level business flow** (wiring diagram) that provides a road map for any changes in the business process.

The Case for Sales and Operations Planning

The Internet is one more innovation that increases the volume and speed of the data your business must react to. To compete, a company must quickly and accurately respond to customer requests. This is only possible if a company understands the capabilities and the status of its supply chain. Successful companies have a structured and disciplined process for creating realistic sales and operations plans that provide a basis for responding to the marketplace.

What is S&OP?

Sales & Operations Planning (S&OP) is a business process that helps to keep demand and supply in balance. In most companies, S&OP is a monthly process. The balancing act starts by looking at the demand at a higher level of aggregation, e.g., product families and groups. Generally, financial targets are developed based on the aggregated information. However, to realize the financial target and determine capacity feasibility, the aggregated demand may need to be broken down to the individual product level.

The ability to see the rise or fall in projected demand allows the business to take appropriate strategic action. If the projected demand shows an increase, capacity can be added, procurement can be planned, and logistics plans can be modified ahead of time. If the projected demand shows a decrease, material procurement can be reduced, and production and logistics plans can be adjusted accordingly.

The focus of S&OP is therefore not only to balance supply and demand but also to *keep them balanced*. It is necessary to have the process in place to do so on a regular basis. The business needs to have early warning capabilities to alert people when and where the process has the potential for getting out of sync. This provides the business an opportunity to develop several options to deal with the impending imbalance and create opportunities to either take advantage of the situation or ward off the disaster.

Proper implementation of an S&OP process at a company will help improve customer service, lower finished goods inventory, stabilize production rates, improve material procurement, and improve teamwork among the management from Sales, Operations, Finance, Customer Service and Information Technology. Indeed the reduced costs sought by those with only a financial view of the world are best achieved in the context of an overall S&OP process.

For successful implementation of S&OP, top management's stewardship and leadership is essential because S&OP affects the Financial Plan and the top management is the owner of that business plan. If the business plan is not adjusted to reflect the new Sales & Operations Plan, there will be a gap between the expected financial result and the forecasts and production plans being used to operate the business.

A business should be managed based on one and only one set of numbers. Senior management's participation emphasizes the importance of integrating operational and financial planning, balancing supply and demand, and enhancing customer service. Senior management's participation and stewardship also encourages functional managers to support the process.

Most of the preparatory work is done by middle management and their staffs earlier in the month. These include forecast updates, data aggregation, identification of production constraints, potential raw material problems and development of various scenarios to be considered by the senior management.

Why Plan?

Supply chain tasks are classified into two broad categories: planning and execution. Execution is best done against an overall plan that takes into account the business strategy and goals. Otherwise, execution degenerates into reactive firefighting activities.

Symptoms of inadequate planning and control and lack of proper communication amongst various business functions include the following:

➢ Missed customer deliveries

➢ Loss of credibility with customers

➢ Lost customers

➢ Expediting

➢ Higher manufacturing costs

➢ Excess Overtime

➢ Premium costs and freight

➢ Reduced flexibility and responsiveness

➢ Higher working capital in inventories

➢ Late new product introductions

➢ Reduced financial performance

"Functional" objectives are often detrimental to the overall business objectives of maximizing the profit margin. Each function might be operating optimally, but because of the conflicting nature of the objectives, organizational synergy is lost. The table below illustrates some of the functional objectives frequently found in a business.

Function	Objective
Sales and Marketing	• Increase sales • Develop new products • Exceed forecasts

Function	Objective
Manufacturing	• Maximize throughput • Minimize costs • Meet quality objectives
Business Management	• Meet revenue goals • Meet corporate financial commitments • Meet price and volume goals
Customer Service	• Maximize availability • Meet every order • Minimize complaints
Inventory Management and Distribution	• Minimize inventory and warehouse costs • Control stocks • Maximize turns • Reduce transport costs

As an example, the objective of the Sales & Marketing organization is to maximize sales and revenue whereas that of the Distribution function is to minimize inventory and warehousing costs. These two competing incentives are at the root of some the problems outlined above. These competing objectives exist for a number of reasons:

- Lack of a well-articulated strategic plan

- Lack of understanding of the "big picture"

- Lack of communication between functions

- An acceptance of "That's the way it's always been done"

- "Stovepipe" information systems designed and implemented to support individual departments or functions

- Management edicts at odds with strategic business needs

- Conflicting performance criteria

- Lack of understanding of how "our" data is used by, or impacts other functions

The purpose of the S&OP process is to get to the root cause of these problems and develop a sound business process to align the strategic and financial objectives with the functional objectives on a routine basis. All the benefits that come from improved demand planning, supply planning, and inventory management are exponentially increased by coordinating these functions to optimize the whole.

Synchronized planning brings about the following benefits:

- Right inventories in right place at right time and lower working capital

- Reduced manufacturing costs (fewer schedule breaks)

- Better coordination of logistics and distribution with manufacturing

- Increased throughput

- Improved customer service

- Improved organizational cooperation and initiative to improve the bottom line

- A new management process to optimize business results.

Business process changes can be made successfully only if management is fully committed to the process. Even with management commitment, change is neither easy nor quick. In our experience, it takes anywhere from six to twelve months to establish an S&OP process that is fully institutionalized, even though benefits are achieved well before then.

Five Steps to Success

The steps described in this chapter are based on work with over 100 companies worldwide. They provide a roadmap for application and business process development based on two observations:

1. In our experience, companies tend to be more successful if they first get control of the tactical supply chain planning and establish a strong S&OP process before addressing finite scheduling and "Capable to Promise" areas. Creating an S&OP framework also facilitates introducing initiatives like lean manufacturing into the organization.

2. Supply Chain Planning technology and Business Process changes should be implemented and institutionalized simultaneously. Introducing technology alone is not usually helpful because it tends to automate ineffective processes. Similarly, business process changes are more easily enforced if they are supported by the required systems and tools so that the planners can immediately practice new ways of doing things.

The road map presented here is a starting point. Because companies may be at different levels of planning sophistication, it may require modification. However, we strongly believe that following the steps outlined here in a disciplined sequence will ultimately shorten the time to achieve a world class planning process.

Each of these steps is specified in terms of goals, tasks, technology requirements, and business process changes. Successful companies approach these steps in a methodical way and use each step as a building block for implementing the final process. This approach not only concentrates organizational effort and resources effectively, it provides a systematic way to increase an organization's supply chain knowledge and maturity.

The improvement is conducted in cycles made up of knowledge acquisition, development of metrics, tool development, and process changes. Lessons learned from each step guide the next.

The overall effort is broken up into a series of six-to-eight week deliverables. Each deliverable provides concrete value to the business, in addition to being a project milestone.

Time is allocated between the steps to institutionalize the changes. There are many real-world constraints that can disrupt an improvement process. Business crises happen from time to time and personnel involved in supply chain planning are often central to resolving these. It is important to recognize that this will happen and provide for these interruptions. For this reason we advocate sufficient time between steps to institutionalize business process changes and train planners in new technology.

Step 1: Understand Customer Demand

The type of demand that a company faces has a major impact on how the supply chain functions. In the extreme case, if the lead time for the majority of orders is less than a day, and it requires more than one day to manufacture and package products, then a pure make-to-order strategy is impractical. Understanding the demand allows the planners to calculate realistic safety stocks and resource buffers in the supply chain.

The demand facing the supply chain is constantly changing. For responsive decision making, the planners must be able to access and analyze the current demand effortlessly. Step 1 is directed to achieving this goal.

Goals:
1. Understand the demand and order stream.
2. Identify the sources of demand variability across customers and products.
3. Put in place metrics for order fulfillment.

Major Tasks:
1. Identify key demand attributes. (Attributes are discussed in detail in a later chapter)
2. Create interfaces and load shipment information from the ERP system at the order/line level of detail.

3. Analyze the shipments information and prepare profiles by the demand attributes for:
    ▪ Order size
    ▪ Order volume
    ▪ Lead time
    ▪ Fill rate

4. Classify customers by number of orders, revenue, lead times, and volume.

5. Classify products by number of orders, revenue, volumes, and lead-time.

6. Determine how the shipment history in the ERP can be used effectively for forecasting, and if it can, then at what level of aggregation.

7. Identify patterns of order placement during the month.

8. Reach agreement on order fulfillment metrics and establish base line.

Technology Deliverables:

1. An easily accessible database that can load shipment and order data from the ERP system on demand.

2. A process to routinely read shipment history. There should be two types of updates: one to read monthly data and another to read the data every day.

3. The ability to graph and report the shipment data. Report examples are:
   - Shipment history with selection by any attribute in the database.
   - Graph open orders versus forecast (if it is available).
   - Revenue and unit shipment reports by any attribute in the database.
   - Percentage of orders filled on time by volume and by orders.

4. Ability to identify significant (by volume or revenue) customer/product combinations.

Supportive Processes:

Processes are perhaps the most important characteristic in sustainable improvements of performance. In this first step however, we're not changing the way people are working, only making more timely information easily available to the extended organization. Experience has shown that this often:

- Creates momentum for improvement, as group managers can easily monitor performance and drill-down into problems in a way that was previously not possible.

- Creates a genuine value for analysis and information sharing.

- Helps provide the analytical capabilities that challenge assumptions people make about their business that directly impact daily execution.

Benefits:

1. The ability to identify specific areas of demand variability, and customer/ product combinations with low customer service, should provide opportunities to reduce late shipments by 20%.

2. The implementation of a metric to measure order fulfillment provides a basis for a continuous improvement process for customer service.

3. If not already known, a quantitative view of the most important customers and product lines can focus business initiatives appropriately for the first time.

Step 2: Analyze Inventories

Inventory is often the most visible aspect of the supply chain because it can be quantified. Together with receivables, it constitutes a key component of the cash-to-cash cycle time. Effective supply chains need to utilize the working capital assigned to them well. The inventories in manufacturing organizations exist to buffer fluctuating demand as well as to buffer manufacturing so that the manufacturing process can run efficiently.

In step 2 the primary goal is to identify whether the existing inventory is positioned to support the supply chain well. To support day to day decisions, planners need to know where inventory is located, how old it is, how accessible it is, and so on. Slow moving stock is damaging on two accounts. First, it ties up working capital, and second it prevents the tied up working capital from being used to support other products.

Goals:
1. Create a process for analyzing inventory to determine how well the inventory supports potential demand.
2. Identify potential excesses or shortfalls.

Major Tasks:
1. Identify the relevant inventory attributes, for example product, package, date produced, amount, warehouse location, and manufacturing location.
2. Put in place a process to refresh the planning database with inventory data on demand from the ERP system.
3. Analyze the inventory in relation to the shipment variability.
4. Identify stocks that are not justified by the demand variability.
5. Identify accumulations of obsolete or off spec inventory.

Technology deliverables:

1. An easily accessible database that can load the inventory data by the agreed upon attributes.

2. A process to routinely read inventory data. The data should include finished, semi-finished, and raw materials.

3. The capability to aggregate and report on inventory by any combination of the defined inventory attributes and to report in terms of inventory volume, value, or days supply.

4. A process to identify gross excesses of inventory and a business process to dispose of these.

Supportive Processes:

1. A process for reviewing inventory imbalances and reallocating inventory.
2. A process for identifying and disposing of aged, obsolete, or sub-quality inventory.

Benefits:

1. Improved visibility of pockets of excess inventory should lead to inventory reductions of 10%.

2. Metrics to measure the inventory "health" provides a basis for a continuous improvement process.

Step 3: Routinely Create a Demand Plan

Establishing a routine demand planning process that operates effectively and efficiently to both collect and predict a company's demand is the next stop on the journey. Identifying the participants in the process, the rules that support the process, and the duration and timing of the process are the key components of the step. However, the resulting process must fit into the overall business planning cycle and support the overall needs of the business as well as the needs of the other planning processes.

Collaborative forecasting is the process for collecting and reconciling the information from diverse sources inside and outside the company to come up with a single unified statement of demand. It consists of four key elements:

- Application of statistics and other algorithms to past data to recover relevant information.

- Processes and systems to collect customer-level input routinely. In some businesses, this may be referred to as geographic information.

- Processes to merge management overrides and inputs with the data collected at the customer level.

- Processes to merge marketing input, which is usually product focused, with the sales view that is usually customer focused.

Part of the demand planning process is to help create a unified statement of the tactical market demand which is accepted by all parts of the organization. Frequently this involves converting the single set of numbers into views that are relevant to each part of the organization. In general there are at least four views that need to be in place to support a demand planning process:

1. A **statistical view** for applying mathematical models. This view is at a level of aggregation where the statistical models provide useful results

2. A **marketing view** that is product family focused. This view is used to input aggregate changes for existing products, new products, handle product substitution, and possibly check for critical components.

3. A **sales view** which is customer focused. It is used to gather customer related information. An example of this view would be a view by region, sales office, and customer.

4. A **manufacturing view** that is used for capacity reconciliation. This would typically be by product or product family, and by week or month.

Step 3 is primarily concerned with implementing a demand planning process with these characteristics.

Goals:
1. Create a demand planning process that can be executed routinely.
2. Institutionalize forecasting metrics.

Major Tasks:
1. Identify the persons or functions that contribute changes to the demand plan.
2. Agree and document the method for creating a single demand plan from different sources like sales, marketing, operations, etc.
3. Identify the required aggregation levels for statistical forecasting.
4. Train and distribute a tool to support collaborative forecasting.
5. Implement forecasting metrics.

Technology deliverables:
1. Software tools to create a demand plan based on a combination of statistical procedures and sales/market input.
2. A process to routinely measure and report on forecast accuracy.
3. The capability to aggregate and report forecasts by any combination of the defined demand attributes.
4. Capability to identify excess inventories based on the demand plan.

Supportive Processes:
1. The most important process improvement is in the promotion of a single demand plan for the organization. Most companies struggle with multiple versions of the forecast resulting in waste and a lack of accountability for operations performance.
2. Implement collaborative processes that include input from all key stakeholders including sales, marketing, pricing, and significant outside customers, together with a defined process to reconcile this information.
3. Clearly define roles and responsibilities.
4. Synchronize demand planning with the annual budget and use the operational forecast as the basis for financial forecasting.

Benefits:
1. A 25% improvement in forecast accuracy, which improves inventory health and customer service.
2. The metrics for measuring forecast accuracy provide a basis for a continuing improvement process.

Required System Characteristics

Often, step 3 requires the installation of a demand planning system. While there are a plethora of commercial systems available, many of them do not have the capability for supporting modern demand planning processes. At a minimum, any selected system should have the following capabilities:

1. Distributed Collection of Input

Forecast inputs are usually gathered from those closest to the customer. These may be the sales persons, customer service representative, or customers themselves. After a forecast input is identified, there is usually an evaluation process. The salesman may check the input against past volume, recent history, accuracy of the customer's past projections before passing on the input for consolidation.

In today's environment, the forecast collection process must be a distributed one, and must allow each sales person to operate independently without being connected directly to the forecasting system. The reason for this is simple: Collecting forecast information is not a central job task of most sales persons. The forecasting system must be able to accommodate different working styles and allow a sales person to operate on his or her local computer for much of the time. Connection to the forecast system is only needed when data needs to be exchanged.

2. Support for Volume and Revenue

For collaborative forecasting to work effectively, the data has to be meaningful to the different organizations involved in creating and reconciling the forecast.

In most organizations revenue projections are key to interpreting sales goals. Marketing and manufacturing, on the other hand, are usually focused on volumes.

The system must be able to accommodate both types of data and maintain the consistency between volume and revenue.

3. Visibility of Forecast Changes

In a collaborative forecasting environment, multiple organizations provide input which is consolidated into the final statement of demand. As the forecast is developed, changes that are made should be visible so that the responsibility and accountability can be maintained.

Consider the situation where a sales person enters a forecast for a customer and product combination. The sales manager reviews and adjusts the total. This is then turned over to marketing for further additions. Rather than change the sales person's forecast, the system must maintain the differences so that the changes made at each organizational level are visible.

What this means is that it is no longer sufficient to merely maintain the previous forecast and use the accuracy of the total forecast as a metric. The forecasting system must maintain and measure the changes made at each organizational level.

Step 4: Balance Supply and Demand

Supply chain planning is all about making planners more productive. You do this by giving them good data, making sure that they are working on the right issues, and providing them with the necessary tools. The purpose of this step is to create a quantitative representation of the supply chain that models the consequences of tactical planning decisions.

The demand view or perspective is usually product or customer focused while the supply view is necessarily resource focused. Choices have to be made when allocating resources to competing products. Without a quantitative tool, there can be no rational allocation process. Decisions are made in favor of the person that shouts the loudest.

While Excel can be a good place to start, we have found that there are some significant issues with Excel-based tools.

- Spreadsheets don't often have the latest data because the data updates from corporate systems are not automated or systemized.

- Setting up a collaborative environment can be difficult because merging spreadsheets can break down into a manual process.

- A number of complex spreadsheets are needed to represent the business problem, and these eventually collapse under their own weight.

- Many of the business rules embedded in the spreadsheets are lost when a planner leaves his or her job.

- Excel lacks the required optimization, simulation and/or statistical tools needed to model the business. To get around this, complex rules of thumb are embedded in the worksheet; unfortunately, these may not be relevant as business conditions change.

- Formats change and considerable manual effort is required to resynchronize the spreadsheets when spreadsheets are passed from one person to another.

For these reasons, a specialized supply chain modeling tool is a prerequisite to step 4.

Goals:

1. Create a model to balance supply and demand.

2. Identify opportunities for optimization.

3. Agree on a suitable horizon for tactical planning.

Major Tasks:

1. Identify manufacturing facilities and the source of capacity information.

2. Create links with the ERP system to routinely update projected receipts, in-transit material, orders, inventory, and other relevant data.

3. Identify manufacturing and distribution constraints.

4. Identify and collect variable costs including material costs, costs, transportation costs (by mode if required), and packaging costs.

5. Collect and quantify margin information.

6. Configure a business model to represent material balance by location (plants, distribution centers, warehouses), and capacity constraints.

Technology Deliverables:

1. A model with sufficient functionality to support supply/demand balancing.

2. A process to routinely test projected demand against capacity at an aggregated level.

3. The capability to report an integrated view of materials requirements, capacity utilization, transport utilization, unmet demand, planned production, projected inventory, and planned transfers.

Supportive Processes:
A well defined process that clearly identifies who is responsible for creating the supply plan, and for providing the capacity and other inputs to the model.
Agreed upon key performance indicators that are focused on business goals, rather than the goals of individual departments.
Clear accountability for the accuracy and timeliness of the data used in the model.

Benefits:
1. A quantitative model to test different demand / supply scenarios.
2. The ability to plan sales, purchasing, manufacturing, and distribution to maximize profit.

Step 5: Implement Sales and Operations Planning (S&OP)

Who is involved in supply chain planning (SCP)? Production planners and schedulers certainly are. However, many others are also directly involved and their needs should be addressed by the S&OP process.

Customers, Customer Service, and Salespersons

This group needs both supply and demand planning information to promise orders accurately. They also affect the plan as they enter orders and initiate deliveries. Salespeople usually forecast–or at least adjust the forecast–for their segment of the business as part of building the demand plan. Many do this with simple forms and spreadsheets, with no way to see historical trends or the impacts their changes have on others. At times of peak production, salespeople need visibility into production to determine whether an "opportunistic" order can be accepted without negative impact to current and planned orders.

Demand Planners

The demand plan is a key component of the S&OP process. This is one of the groups that traditionally use demand-planning packages. Their ability to generate a demand plan is enhanced if they can access and consolidate the changes made by customers, customer service, and salespersons quickly. Conversely, to keep the demand plan synchronized with the business plan, the demand planners need to view the S&OP outputs so that they can make the necessary modifications to the planned demand.

Marketing Personnel

Many of marketing's initiatives are designed to drive demand. Their input is needed so that the S&OP process can project the impact of promotions, price initiatives, and new product introductions on the overall demand plan. Further, they need to track actual results against expectations to allocate budget effectively and recommend product line and mix strategies. Optimization tools can facilitate promotions planning with decision support for both "when" and "what type" of promotion mix to run for each segment. For them, the results of the S&OP process provide information on available capacity and resources that can be used to support marketing initiatives.

Production Planners

Production planners are at the heart of the S&OP process because they are central to balancing demand and supply. It is usually their responsibility to gather the routine inputs, prepare alternatives for management, and distribute the production requirements to manufacturing. As such, this group is one of the most common users of supply chain planning systems and should participate actively in all phases of the S&OP process.

In many organizations, this group also takes on the role of the S&OP coordinator

Transport Planners

Inbound and outbound logistics can be a key determinant of schedule and cost adherence. Yet in most companies, transportation is planned relatively independently of demand planning and production planning. This is detrimental to the S&OP process because:

- Logistics plays an increasingly more significant role in order fulfillment because of the reliance on outsourced manufacturing.

- The emphasis on using returnable containers means that transportation assets (containers, pallets, railcars, etc) need to be managed so that they are available at production facilities when they are needed.

- Fluctuating energy prices can have a large impact on the supply chain. These costs can be mitigated by using inventory and other resources adroitly.

S&OP Coordinator

Companies that perform an S&OP process well, usually have a person responsible for bringing the parties together and then rationalizing the varied inputs to create a sales and operations plan for the organization. In many companies, this is still a matter of reviewing reams of documents in different formats, each based on independently calculated plans and inconsistent data. The job of the S&OP coordinator can be made easier if there is an integrated tool set to bring together demand, production, inventory, and transportation management data.

Financial Analysts

The S&OP process is designed to create and maintain an operational plan for the business. As such it should be used as the basis for short term financial projections and cash requirements.

Beyond the various formats with inconsistent data, there are often gaps in understanding cost structures based on myopic views. The financial analysts are responsible for reviewing the cost and margin information used in the S&OP process to ensure that the numbers are consistent with the company's projections.

Business Managers

Executives for an enterprise, line of business, or division normally have some relatively straightforward goals for profitability, customer delivery fill rates and satisfaction, and process improvement. Very often, these managers rely on detailed yet filtered data and reports that each departmental manager feeds in from a particular viewpoint. This does not match their need for high-level unbiased information on which to make sound decisions.

Because the S&OP process represents a single consolidated view of operations, business managers should use it to achieve their operational objectives. In fact business objectives should drive the S&OP process, and the S&OP metrics should measure performance against business objectives.

Inventory Planners

In many organizations, there may in fact be no designated role called "inventory planner". Where such a role does exist, the inventory planners have a challenging task because they neither control the supply which adds to the inventory, nor do they control the demand which depletes inventory.

For inventory planning to be effective, it needs to be done in conjunction with planning demand and supply. The S&OP process is the logical forum for setting and implementing inventory policies because it provides a central place for balancing the inputs and outputs to inventory, as well as monitoring the working capital tied up in inventory.

Suppliers

Materials suppliers and contract manufacturing partners are a major element of any company's ability to balance supply with demand. While contracts set in advance the resources that are committed by the contract manufacturer or supplier, today's uncertain markets often make these established levels inappropriate.

If strategic suppliers are given visibility into the S&OP process, they can often the additional flexibility and responsiveness needed to react to market demand.

A word of caution: if the internal processes are not disciplined and effective, it is not effective to expose the S&OP process to external suppliers. Many companies confuse data transfers with collaboration. Providing information that is unreliable often confuses the suppliers and in fact damages the supplier relationship.

Goals:
1. Put in place a structured process to routinely plan supply chain operations and reconcile the operations with financial goals.
2. Define the interfaces from planning to schedule execution.

Major Tasks:
1. Incorporate additional business constraints identified in step 4 into the supply model.
2. Identify and create sufficient reports to support the S&OP process.
3. Test the interfaces from planning to scheduling.
4. Provide the necessary business process training to implement S&OP.

Technology Deliverables:
1. A model that can be routinely used for supply/demand balancing at an aggregate level. This includes creating any automatic data interfaces and scenario analysis capability.
2. Sufficient reports to support a monthly S&OP function.

Supportive Processes:
1. A disciplined process, timetable, and team to conduct routine S&OP for the business
2. A defined process for reconciling the S&OP plan with financial objectives.

Benefits:
1. A 1-2% reduction in operating cost.
2. An operational plan that maximizes margins.
3. A process to quickly handle demand and/or supply disruptions by providing a quantitative model as the basis for evaluating them.
4. A quantitative process to determine if and when new demand should be accepted.
5. A tool for evaluating planned changes to markets, sourcing patterns, capacity, process technology, and the distribution network improvements.

Organizing Supply Chain Data

Describing the Supply Chain

The largest volume of data that a Supply Chain Manager usually deals with is the customer demand. Customer demand for products drives decisions across all supply chain functions: sales, marketing, purchasing, manufacturing, and distribution. Understanding the company's demand stream is a fundamental step to improving supply chain performance.

Why don't companies do this routinely? Some do, but most companies are stymied by two related problems. First, the available data is at a transaction level of detail, describing individual shipments and orders. It is hard to get useful business insights by looking directly at this highly detailed data. Secondly, people are so busy doing their day to day jobs that they don't have the time to manually manipulate this detailed data into useful information.

Identifying Data Attributes

The historical data stored in an ERP system contains a wealth of information. In order to mine it effectively, we need to determine how to view it. The challenge is that the different business functions in a company get value from different views of this data. Sales needs a customer-oriented perspective, manufacturing has a product focus, and distribution is interested in modes of transport.

These different requirements are achievable. Despite that, some companies try to simplify the process of working with data by insisting that everybody use the same view. If the different business functions are able to agree on what that should be, it is often so detailed that it is too cumbersome for anyone to use.

In order to support these different views, we need to know the attributes of data that are relevant to the different business functions. We use these attributes to aggregate, or "slice and dice," the detailed data into views that provide useful information to the different business functions. Modern software tools allow users to also translate from one view to another consistently.

Draw the Product Structure

The easiest way to understand the product structure do this is to draw a simple picture, as shown below.

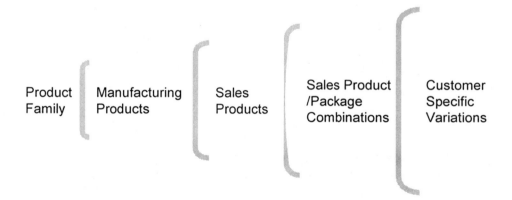

The highest level of the product hierarchy shown above is the product family. Each product family contains multiple manufacturing products. Each manufacturing product has one internal identifier, which usually defines the production process and product composition. Each manufacturing product may have multiple sales product identifiers (this is usually done for pricing purposes). Each sales product is sold in multiple product/package combinations. There are also multiple customer specific specifications associated with each sales product/package.

This example shows that you may need more than just a product identifier to identify what was shipped to a customer. In this example, you need the sales product/package plus the customer specification. Since this can create opportunities for confusion, many companies create a unique product identifier for every set of customer specific specifications.

Many process industry and consumer packaged goods companies have this type of product hierarchy.

Draw the Demand Structure

Our next step is to draw a picture of the hierarchy used to define demand. This may be tied to the customer, a geographical region, or some combination. An example is shown below.

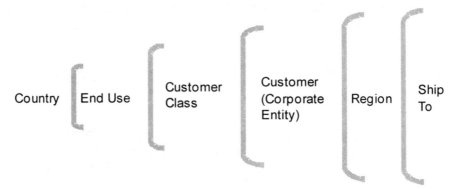

The highest level in our example is the country the demand is coming from. There may be multiple end uses associated with each country. Within each industry group, three customer classes exist (A, B, and C). These classes are often based on current annual revenues and future potential. Each class has multiple corporate entities that are customers. One of these customers may buy product in multiple geographic regions, and each region may have multiple locations that product is shipped to for that customer.

As you create these drawings, look for any exceptions to the defined segmentation and hierarchy.

Other Supply Chain Views

Most businesses have defined product structures, along with a hierarchy for describing the geographical distribution of demand. Other relevant attributes vary with the details of the business, and the capabilities of the systems that store data.

Sales often want views of history or forecast that correspond to the structure of the sales organization. The attributes listed below are a typical example. The highest level would be a Business Manager or VP of Sales. They may be responsible for multiple sales regions, and each sales region may have multiple sales persons. Each sales person has multiple accounts.

Sales VP   Sales region   Sales Representative

Depending on the particular business, it may also be important to outline a manufacturing hierarchy, a financial hierarchy, and a distribution hierarchy.

Some customers may specify a particular plant, production line, warehouse, distribution center, or mode of transport. This is quite different from the "customer specific variations" discussed in the product hierarchy. Customers may specify a transport lane because of political or cost reasons that have nothing to do with the product characteristics.

This information is also useful for manufacturing and distribution planning, so you may want to include some or all of the following attributes for each shipment.

1. Warehouse or distribution center
2. Transport mode
3. Manufacturing location
4. Production line

The remaining attributes of interest usually define how much was shipped, when it was shipped, and the revenues the shipment produced. The data available will vary with the order management system being used. Virtually all systems have the quantity shipped, and the order quantity.

1. Shipped quantity
2. Order quantity
3. Order placement date
4. Requested ship date
5. First promised ship date
6. Current scheduled ship date
7. Actual ship date
8. Date of receipt
9. Flag on whether order is open or has shipped
10. Flag on whether order is for an internal or external customer
11. Price
12. Discount
13. Rebate or deal code
14. Invoice amount

The information on the ship date varies with the capabilities of the order management system, and the way in which the system was implemented. Ideally, you want to capture the date the order was placed, the date first requested by the customer, the first promised ship date, the current scheduled ship date, the actual ship date, and the date of receipt. Capturing the date the order was placed lets you analyze customer lead times. The requested, first promised date, current scheduled date, and actual ship date are used to analyze customer service performance. The date of receipt is used to analyze customer service and the performance of transport providers.

Unfortunately, many order management systems do not provide enough fields to capture all of these dates. In addition, sometimes these systems are implemented so that an entry on one field automatically overwrites another field. You need to determine what information is available, and also what data is valid. Don't assume that data is valid just because there are entries in a field.

Most order systems will have a flag or status code that indicates whether an order has been shipped. The order system also will usually indicate whether a shipment is an internal transfer or sale, or a sale to an external customer. Be sure to capture both internal and external shipments because to forecast external demand, we may need to remove internal shipments including shipments to distributors from the data.

The attributes that define the revenue associated with a shipment can vary greatly, both in terms of the options available and the way these options are used. A product price and the invoice amount are usually readily available. The information that defines any discount given from standard prices, such as a discount amount or a rebate or deal code, can be more difficult to obtain and interpret.

System Selection Implications

Once the interesting attributes have been identified, companies usually face a choice. If they can agree to a single well defined hierarchy, then the demand planning solution offered by the ERP vendor is usually sufficient. Otherwise, you will need to consider a system whose architecture allows you to create hierarchies dynamically so that different people can look at the demand data in the way that they are used to.

Performance Implications

There is no free lunch. As you increase the number of attributes, you increase the volume of data that you are working with. You also potentially increase the number of combinations and permutations your tools have to work across in analyzing this data. Both of these factors can increase the time required to generate the views that you want, and to analyze data.

We don't want to arbitrarily restrict the numbers of attributes that you use, but it is important to make sure that those attributes are valid. You don't want to penalize performance by manipulating data that is not useful. It is common to find demand attributes that are obsolete, redundant, have been abandoned, or are used inconsistently. This is particularly true if the system storing the demand data has been in place for more than 1 or 2 years.

In our experience, a business can usually describe its data accurately with between 20 and 30 attributes. These are sufficient to generate views for most relevant supply chain functions across a company.

Using the Attributes

Each shipment or invoice line item should be logically tied to each of these attributes. It is entirely possible that a particular shipment record does not possess a value for an attribute. For example, an internet sale may not have a sales person assigned to it. In this case, that shipment record should have an attribute value of "Not Specified" for each attribute.

The system being used to analyze this data should be able to dynamically summarize the raw data by any selection and filtering of the attributes. It is important that the users be allowed to specify the selection, filtering, and view dynamically. Pre-configured reports are useful only if you know what question to ask. Frequently, the question that the users want answers to are determined by the situation and business context they are in at that time.

Using Data for Forecasting

You can apply statistical techniques to any data, but the results may not be useful. As you increase the level of detail at which you are forecasting, the prediction becomes less accurate. The converse is also true, that as you aggregate data, random errors tend to cancel each other out and the prediction becomes more accurate. However, the level of precision of the results may not be useful for the intended purpose.

This section presents some rules of thumb (based on our collective experience) for applying statistical techniques. Highly aggregated forecasts are not very useful for planning capacity or production, but you can use recent history to add detail back to an aggregated forecast. We will describe how this is done in the next section.

Rules of Thumb for Aggregation

There are a number of dimensions over which you can aggregate historical data.

- Time periods
- Customers
- Product/package combinations, or products

History is most commonly aggregated over time periods. Even though many businesses want to see demand on a weekly basis, statistical forecasting techniques are still most commonly applied to monthly data.

If the distribution network is large and complex, you may consider aggregating customers by the geographical region that they are in, and/or the mode of transport they most commonly use.

It is also common to aggregate product/package combinations to the product level. In industries with short product life cycles, such as the semiconductor industry, demand may be aggregated to a product family level, where the family designation defines how manufacturing capacity is consumed.

Defining the proper level of aggregation is an exploratory process. You need to examine different views of the data, and actually apply statistical methods to different views of the data.

We will use the phrase "market segment" to identify a combined customer and product aggregation that you are considering. Here are some rules of thumb for defining the aggregated market segments and time periods to use for forecasting.

- Less than 40% of the number of time periods for a market segment should have a demand of zero. Many statistical techniques will not work well if 40% of the values are zero.

- Be wary of any market segment with zero values for recent time periods.

- If a trend or seasonality is clearly visible when you plot the data, the data should be usable for forecasting.

- Ideally, there should be at least 4 to 6 orders (observations) in each time bucket for each market segment.

- No element in the grouping for a market segment should have more than 25% of the total demand. If a customer or product has more than 25%, they should be forecast separately.

Adding Detail to an Aggregated Forecast

Recent history can be used to add detail back to a statistical forecast. This is done by developing profiles for the areas in which you want to add detail, and then scaling the forecast by those profiles. This is most commonly done to convert from a monthly view of demand to a weekly view, and to convert a product level forecast to a forecast for product/package combinations. The same approach can be used to add detail on geographical distribution and modes of transport.

Create Profiles

Most businesses see some regular cycle of demand across the month, based on the manufacturing and inventory policies of their customers. The month may be front ended loaded, back end loaded, or peak during the month. We can use this regular pattern to distribute a demand forecast for a larger period, like a month, over a shorter period of time.

Plot the weekly profile of demand for a cross section of products for the last month, the last quarter, and for the last year. Decide which profile you want to use. Normalize the profiles by dividing by mean monthly demand. This gives you the coefficients to use in converting monthly demand to weekly demand.

Repeat this for order size or package type (which ever makes sense for your business. Plot profiles of demand by order size or package type by month, by quarter, and by year. Decide which profile you want to use. Normalize the profiles by dividing by total demand over the time period you are plotting. You now have the coefficients for converting a forecast at the product level to a forecast of package/product combinations.

Using Data for Inventory Analysis

The attributes used to identify the inventory should be at a detailed enough level so that each component of inventory can be treated as homogenous product. For example, if a product is matched to an order using size, speed of chip, or other specification, then this needs to be included as an inventory attribute.

For this reason, it is preferable to extract the inventory data by lot. The reason for this is that in many situations, lot level specifications are used to determine if the product can be shipped to specific customers.

The inventory attributes may include *product description attributes* like Manufacturing plant, key ingredient, package, product specifications, date of manufacture, etc. and *location attributes* like warehouse, location within a warehouse and so on.

The following table summarizes the data that will normally be required to support Inventory analysis.

Data Category	Description	Fields
Shipment History	Daily shipment transactions for raw material supply from vendors, Intercompany shipments such as raw materials from plant to plant and finished goods shipments to warehouses and customers.	• Product • Shipment date • Demand location (ship from location) Arrival date • Supply location (ship to location) • Shipment quantity • Fitted forecast quantity

Data Category	Description	Fields
Forecast History	Actual forecast quantities by location by product by customer	• Product • Date of forecast • Demand location • Forecast quantity • Customer if applicable
Lead time History	Daily shipment transactions for raw material supply from vendors. Intercompany shipments such as raw materials from plant to plant and finished goods shipments to warehouses and customers.	• Product • Source • Destination • Mode of transport • Order date and time • Receipt date and time
Production variance including Unplanned outages	The daily amount of finished goods that was scheduled, and the actual amount that was produced at a plant.	• Plant • Date of production • Product • Planned production • Actual production
Consumption History	The daily amount of raw material that was scheduled, and the actual amount that was used at a plant.	• Plant • Product • Date • Planned Consumption • Actual Consumption

Data Category	Description	Fields
Locations: Plant DC Customer Warehouse Vendors End Customers	This will contain a list of locations that contain vendors, plants, terminals, managed customer locations, and end customers.	• Code • Description
$/Unit Conversion Factors	This will define the values to be used in converting volume to dollars.	• Product • Location • $ Value
Customer Segmentation	This will identify the customer segment for each customer by volume.	• Customer • Customer segment

Analyzing Inventory Data

In order to match the inventory to demand, it is necessary to determine the common attributes that describe demand and the inventory. In other words, if the demand attributes *are product, package, customer, ship-from warehouse*, and the inventory attributes are *product, manufacturing plant, package, and location*, then the common attributes are *product, package, and location*. (For the rest of this discussion, we will assume that these are the common attributes.)

It is useful to have a tool to slice and dice the information to answer the following types of questions:

• Is there a large difference in "days of supply" for the same product-package combination at different warehouses?

• Is the inventory significantly older at one or more warehouse?

- Sort the products by descending demand. Plot the percentage of inventory by product against the percentage of demand for that product. For example, the highest moving product may constitute 30% of the volume, but only 20% of the inventory. Is this how you would like to run the supply chain? Are there significant differences in this plot from one warehouse to another?

- For critical raw materials, estimate the consumption based on the finished product demand. How many days supply of the critical raw material do we have in stock?

Identifying Aged Inventory

Days of Supply (DOS) versus Inventory Velocity (IV)

The Days of Supply (DOS) measurement is commonly used to measure supply chain efficiency. Its calculation has the three elements that are needed for a metric to be successful:

1. It is easy to understand and easy to calculate.

2. It suggests a direction for improvement; either it is too high or too low.

3. It provides an aggregated view.

While useful in measuring total inventory volume, DOS does not provide a good indication showing how well the inventory matches demand at the aggregate level.

Item	Monthly Demand	Inventory	DOS
A	50	25	15
B	5	20	120
Total	55	45	25

For example, in the example, Item A and Item B are in the same **family**. The DOS for the **family** is 25 (45/55*30). However, the inventory is clearly unbalanced.

The **percentage of inventory projected to be consumed in the next forecast interval, or Inventory Velocity (IV)**, is a much better measure of how well the inventory matches demand. The total amount expected to be consumed in the next month is 25 units of item A and 5 units of item B for a total of 30 units. The aggregate inventory velocity is (30/45) or 66.7%.

Item	Monthly Demand	Inventory	DOS	Inventory Velocity (IV)
A	50	25	15	100%
B	5	20	120	25%
Total	55	45	25	66.7%

Now consider the case where the same inventory is distributed better between the products. The total inventory is the same, as is the DOS.

Item	Monthly Demand	Inventory	DOS	Inventory Velocity (IV)
A	50	30	18	100%
B	5	15	90	33%
Total	55	45	25	77.8%

However in this case, a larger fraction of the physical inventory, 78%, will be consumed within the next month because the inventory matches the demand more closely.

Practical Considerations for Using Inventory Velocity (IV)

All Stock Keeping Units (SKU) cannot be treated equally. Production, lot size, and other restrictions have an impact on inventory levels. To address this, it is useful to classify SKU's into categories—each with its own Inventory Velocity. Products made in response to a customer request and high volume products made continuously should have an Inventory Velocity close to 100%.

Products that are slow moving but with short lead times usually have a much lower Inventory Velocity.

The appropriate Inventory Velocity (IV) is frequently a function of the supply chain. Products made once a year, for example, should have a target IV considerably lower than those made once a month. For this reason, while it is useful to look at IV as an aggregate measure, it is important to recognize that IV by groups of similar products is a better indicator.

Our experience indicates that typical IV for chemical operations is in the 60 to 70% range. Well run supply chains have an IV between 75 and 85%. Anything higher usually indicates a make-to-order environment or frequent product shortages. Similarly, a supply chain with an IV below 60% usually has frequent product shortages and shipment delays because this usually indicates that the inventory is positioned in the wrong products.

Alternate Products

In many situations, some products can be substituted for others with relatively little effort: for example, a faster semi-conductor chip for a slower one, a higher-grade product for a lower one, one package type for another, and for sheet products, a slightly wider roll for a narrower one. Therefore, the amount of a product that is likely to be consumed in the next forecast period also depends on how easily it can substitute for other products.

Let's illustrate this through an example:

Product	Monthly Demand	Inventory
A	50	25
B	5	20
C	20	5
Total	75	50

Product C has a demand of 20, but product B can be substituted for C. In this case, the IV for our example is 100% because all the excess for B can be consumed by the demand for C.

In actual practice, the IV is usually calculated by means of a simple Linear Program (LP) that represents the substitution rules. However, the example above illustrates why a simple DOS calculation may not suggest the right inventory strategy or direction.

Alternate Locations

Inventory needs to be at the right place to satisfy customer demand. In a global business, inventory of an SKU located in Singapore is unlikely to be used to satisfy a demand in Cleveland. However, the inventory in Columbus or even in Atlanta might be expedited readily.

Just as alternate products can be considered in calculating Inventory Velocity, alternate locations can also be rolled into the calculation. In such a case, inventory at an alternate location is treated as an alternate product. Not only will analyzing the inventory in this way provide a metric, but it will also provide a mechanism to identify inventory imbalances that can be directly addressed.

Another useful analysis with IV is netting the demand from inventory at the product level. If you sort this data in descending order, you have the entire slow moving inventory. You can not focus on fixing all the inventory problems overnight; therefore, this Pareto list of slow movers is the place to start. You could set a target of working on the top 10 slow movers each month. Of course, it is also helpful to track each month to see how many repeaters from earlier months make your 10 list.

Improving the Business Processes

Regardless of whether a formal, recognized planning process exists or not, every company is doing some planning. Identifying the existing process, documenting the procedure, and understanding the various interactions can provide a great deal of information into how the business is organized and how it views the supply chain planning process. This exercise is also quite useful in identifying potential barriers and issues.

Documenting the Current State

Documenting the current process need not be an extended and painful exercise. After all, the purpose is to identify areas for improvement areas – not to create a definitive documentation for every process. The process and checklist below have been successful in many situations.

Current Planning Process

1. Draw a diagram identifying the main steps and people that are involved in generating the operational demand.

2. How many people are involved in the process? Identify each person as **accountable,** or **responsible**.

Demand Planning Step	Responsible	Accountable
Collect data and verify		
Generate statistical forecasts		
Ensure collaborative inputs (if any) are timely		
Reconcile inputs to the forecast		
Distribute demand plan		
Monitor forecasts against shipments/orders/invoices		

3. Repeat the same analysis for the process that creates a supply plan.

Supply Planning Step	Responsible	Accountable
Collect data for production constraints including planned shutdowns.		
Modify the supply plan to accommodate the demand plan and updated supply constraints.		
Develop and review alternative supply options		
Provide feedback to demand planners about supply issues.		
Prepare the plan for the S&OP review meeting		

4. Is there clear accountability for generating the demand plan, the sales plan, and the supply plan at regular intervals?

5. Is there clear accountability for the quality of the demand and supply plan?

Current Planning Cycle

1. Is there a monthly cycle around which the operational plan will be generated?

2. List any key dates in the planning process.

3. What is the current planning horizon?

Current Demand and Supply Plan

1. How often is a new plan generated?

2. Who generates the plan?

3. Who reviews it, and who provides changes?

4. Is the demand plan changed during the month? If so, how and by whom?

5. Is the supply and distribution plan changed during the month? If so, how and by whom?

6. Does manufacturing modify the supply plan before it is published?

7. Is the operations plan compared to the annual budget or "profit objective"?

8. What is the time horizon of the budget?

9. Are any statistical methods used in generating the forecast? Are any analytical tools used in creating the supply plan?

10. Is the forecast generated by product/sold-to combination or at a more aggregated level?

11. Is there any forecast generated for purchased items or semi-finished requirements?

12. How is performance measured against the plan? Are metrics distributed?

Data and Systems

1. How and where are the plans stored?

2. Are the plans in the current system updated every day or periodically?

Designing the New Process

To design a relevant process, some key questions need to be answered. Often it is useful to structure a workshop session with key participants to get a common understanding. The business needs to have a common agreement on the questions below.

Supply/Demand Balancing Interaction

1. What is the level of aggregation at which supply and demand are to be balanced?

2. Do the plans need to be reported at other aggregations?

3. Is there a need to consolidate orders received every day with the current sales?

4. How often should the demand plan be communicated to the supply/demand balancing function? How often should changes to the supply plan be communicated?

5. Is there a need to flag orders that are "out of the normal pattern of variability"? For example, the business may want to identify major changes in a customer's order pattern.

6. Does the capacity feasible sales plan need to be fed back to the demand manager? (In some industries, capacity is relatively flexible and does not represent a constraint on the plan.)

7. Are there triggers that can be identified which will prompt a revision to the plans?

Sales Interaction

1. Do the sales persons need to provide input to the demand management process?

2. Is there a requirement for asynchronous input?

3. Does the sales management need to review the plan?

4. Does the sales management need to change the plan?

5. Do we want to track bookings and orders separately from shipments?

6. What kind of aggregated views are required for sales?

Marketing Interaction

1. How often are new products introduced?

2. How often are products eliminated?

3. Are there frequent price changes and/or promotions?

4. How are promotions planned?

5. Is there a promotions calendar that is available?

6. Does marketing override the demand plan at the lowest level or at an aggregation?

Output Data

1. What metrics are to be used initially to judge the plans?

2. What are the initial reporting requirements?

3. Is there a need for maintaining multiple forecast versions? (For example, last month's forecast, etc.)

4. Is there a need to track forecast and supply performance against the budget as part of S&OP process? While this is desirable in most cases, there are instances where the budget is developed at such an aggregated level that it may be impossible to compare the numbers with the S&OP outputs.

Miscellaneous Review Items for Supporting Systems

1. Adding and deleting "New" Items to Database. It is often inconvenient to add new items to the ERP because complete information may not be available. However, there is a need to create a placeholder so that demand for the new item can be forecast.

2. Establishing the period-end process – fully automated vs. partially interactive.

3. How to measure & track forecast errors, and the performance of forecast analysts.

4. Authority levels by user type (security)

5. The process and tools to be used to incorporate sales person's input

6. Whether or not the S&OP data is to be shared with key accounts

7. The extent to which Customer Forecasts are to be included in the demand statement. Customer forecasts are not always reliable. They represent one source of information but this information has to be filtered before it is included in the plan.

8. Distribution of print reports

9. How the plans are to be archived, and for how long.

10. Proper application of statistical forecast models

11. Is the process going to enforce a frozen period for entering data?

12. Use of mid-period adjustments

13. What kind of granularity is to be used for the S&OP. Frequently, shorter periods like weeks or months are used for the immediate future, and quarters further out.

14. Define levels of aggregation and how these aggregation levels will be used

15. Define number of years of demand history. The demand history will need to be filtered for obsolete products, customers, and other

attributes to make it useful. For this reason, it is not always useful to get all the available historical data.

16. Identify the systems and automation tools to be used to support S&OP

17. The methods to be used for blending various forecast inputs into a consensus plan.

   a. What business rules will be used to consolidate collaborative inputs?

      a. None – all inputs accepted and incorporated at face value

      b. Last update overrides all previous inputs, marketing/sales/product

      c. Managers review all inputs and provide consolidated forecast

      d. Other

   b. What business process will be used to resolve conflicts that may occur in collaborative forecasting process?

Extending Participation

Collaboration requires clear articulation of business rules, override acceptance rules, timing of posting the changes to customer and receiving the customer input.

Collaboration with Sales Reps

1. How many Sales Reps by region/location will be involved with Collaboration?

2. How do they currently participate in the forecasting process (e.g. review forecasts – responsible for providing customer level forecasts, provide ad hoc customer updates)?

3. What is the desired role for the sales reps in the forecasting process and what type of interactive goal is foreseen in the

process between the sales reps and the Demand planners (global or regional)? How often will sales reps need to enter updates, adjustments or overrides?

4. What types of forecast related data and at what level of detail would the sales reps like to see? Data often includes history, forecast, and orders. Levels can vary from product family to detailed SKU, with possible additions of customer dependent information.

5. At what level of forecast detail should sale reps enter overrides or updates? (E.g. low level of detail - customer, product-package, ship to location, or at higher level of detail – customer, product.)

6. How often will they need to enter in updates, adjustments or overrides? Is there a monthly cycle envisioned? Is there a fixed time in the month when they will be required to provide updates/overrides?

7. Who will approve the overrides and updates provided by sales reps? What basis will be used for the approval process?

8. How should the sales reps interact with the collaborative forecast application and why? These include web based interfaces, local applications on their computer, corporate database systems, existing sales force automation systems or others. What interaction mechanisms will not be acceptable or have failed in the past?

9. What types of access security/authorizations will be required? Should sales reps only be able to view/update data for their pre-assigned customers? Should they be able to see all but only enter overrides for some?

10. How much accountability do/should the sales reps have for the accuracy of the forecast?

11. What incentives do/should the sales reps have for improving forecast accuracy?

Collaboration with Marketing/Product Managers

1. How many Marketing/Product managers by region/location will be involved with collaboration?

2. How do they currently participate in the forecasting process (e.g. review forecasts – responsible for providing customer level forecasts provide ad hoc customer updates, other)?

3. What is the desired role for the Marketing/Product managers in the forecasting process and what type of interaction is foreseen in the "to be" process between them and the Demand planners (global or regional)?

4. What types of forecast related data and at what level of detail would they like to see? (e.g. History, Forecast, Orders, Product family level, detailed SKU or SAP material code number level, aggregate by marketing/sales region, product, other types of data of interest)

5. At what level of forecast detail should they enter overrides or updates? (e.g. low level of detail – customer, product-package, ship to location, or at higher level of detail – total market, total region – all customers by product family)

6. How often will they need to enter updates, adjustments or overrides? Is there a monthly cycle envisioned - e.g. is there a fixed time in the month when they will be required to provide updates/overrides?

7. Who will approve the overrides and updates provided? What basis will be used for the approval process?

8. How should they interact with the collaborative forecast application and why? (Web based interface, local application on their computer, corporate database system, existing sales force automation system – AME, other) What interaction mechanisms will not be acceptable or have failed in the past?

9. How much accountability do/should they have for the accuracy of the forecast?

10. What incentives do/should they have for improving forecast accuracy?

Collaboration with Customers

1. How many customers by region/location will be involved with collaboration?

2. What criterion should be used to select or identify customers that should participate in the collaborative forecasting process (e.g. variability, past forecast accuracy, volume)?

3. Are there currently any mechanisms/processes for customers to provide future demand information (E-Mail, fax, EDI, phone calls)?

4. What is the desired role for the customers in the forecasting process and what type of interaction is foreseen in the "to be" process between them and the Demand planners (global or regional)?

5. What types of forecast related data and at what level of detail would be appropriate to make available to customers? (e.g. History, Forecast, Orders, other types of data of interest)

6. At what level of forecast detail should they enter overrides or updates? (e.g. product-package, ship to location, monthly, weekly, other)

7. How often should they provide updates, adjustments or overrides? Is there a monthly cycle envisioned - e.g. is there a fixed time in the month when they will be required to provide updates/overrides?

8. Who will approve the overrides and updates provided by the customers? What basis will be used for the approval process?

9. How should they interact with the collaborative forecast application and why? What interaction mechanisms will not be acceptable or have failed in the past?

10. What incentives do/should customers have for improving their forecast accuracy?

11. Do you currently have any VMI customers?

12. What data is obtained from the VMI customers (e.g. inventory, projected consumptions)? How the data is received, processed, and used?

13. What data information is fed back to VMI customers and how (E-Mail, web, other)?

Implementation Considerations

Implementation steps will vary from one company to another but there are some key principles to bear in mind:

Accountability

In successful S&OP processes, three roles need to be filled. These are the demand planner, the supply planner, and the S&OP coordinator. One person can often fill two of these roles. In some situations, the S&OP coordinator also fills the demand planning or supply planning role, but we have not encountered any successful process where a single individual fills all three roles. There needs to be a check and balance function provided by the involvement of a second person for at least one of the three roles.

The demand planner is responsible for creating a statistical forecast if necessary, distributing the initial demand plan to groups that are to provide input, collecting the input, and consolidating the inputs into a single demand plan. The supply planner is responsible for identifying resource bottlenecks, disruptions to capacity, creating a consensus on actual manufacturing and distribution capacity, and communicating the supply plan.

Transparency

For the S&OP process implementation to be successful there must be transparency of the data as well as the results. The shipment and forecast data, together with the manufacturing inputs and the operations, plan should be made available to the participants so that they can analyze and report on it. While static reports are useful, we have found that giving participants a slice and dice capability and an on-line window into the data can help to increase participation

In addition, the mechanism for including overrides in the final plan should be documented and made available. Lastly, the demand plan must be made available so that participants in the process can view and aggregate it in ways that make sense to them.

Efficiency

To be effective, a supply chain planning process must collect information efficiently. What this means is that sales persons (or others who are expected to provide input) must be asked only for significant changes without having to review every product for every account every month. It is the demand planner's responsibility to separate the "significant few" from the "trivial many".

Similarly, for capacity inputs or other routinely needed data, the process of acquiring the data should be automated as much as possible. Normally this is most effectively done by creating a unified supply chain planning database that acts as a data consolidator and repository.

Consistency

Regular planning should be executed on a routine basis so that it becomes a natural part of a person's job. Appropriate procedures should be set up to disseminate the plan on a regular basis.

Modeling the Supply Chain

"…all models are wrong, but some are useful" – Albert Einstein

Every company is unique. Although most companies have some level of activity in sales, purchasing (or procurement), manufacturing, and distribution, the relative importance and complexity of these areas will vary from one company to the next. A semiconductor company may have very complex manufacturing but simple distribution, while a company selling consumer goods may be very distribution intensive. Companies also tend to evolve their own language for describing supply chain activities. This language is influenced by the industry the company is in; its products, organizational structure, production and distribution activities, and history. Understanding the business and its various dimensions is the key to a successful supply planner development.

The goal of creating a model to balance supply and demand is to:

- Decide when to procure raw or intermediate materials

- Decide where to source production, either with internal capacity or via purchases

- Project movements of intermediates between manufacturing sites

- Define sourcing and inventory policies on the distribution network. Policies specify alternative modes of transport, and when they are to be triggered, inventory targets, and the circumstances under which the re-planning is to occur.

In creating the Planning Engine key business restrictions have to be taken into account. The goal at this stage is to build an *adequate* representation of the business, but not necessarily a *comprehensive* representation. A simple model is more readily understood and provides better value in use.

While a spreadsheet model is often used to quantify the relationship between demand and supply, our experience is that these models tend to become overly complex and unmanageable.

Methodology

Linear Programming (LP) is a powerful technique for addressing many real world issues. It was first used successfully during the Second World War for optimizing military tactics. Since then, it has been widely applied to a variety of business problems. The technique is especially well suited to sales and operations planning because it allows material balance and capacity issues to be modeled simply and effectively.

Consider a manufacturer making 2 products, using 3 ingredients on 2 machines. Product 1 is sold for $18 per unit and product 2 is sold for $10 per unit. If each product takes the same amount of each ingredient to make, and also consumes the same machine resources, then it is clear that the manufacturer should maximize the production of Product 1.

However, in practice products usually consume ingredients in different ratios. If product 1 requires 3 units of ingredient 1 and product 2 requires 1 unit, then this may not be a good choice because three times as much of product 2 can be made with the same resource.

A supply chain planning model usually has the following components

Model Component	Example
Decision Variables	These are real-world activities whose values we need to know. An example is the amount of a product that needs to be manufactured in a certain period.
Time Horizon	The period for which the model is planning. This could be 6 months or 5 years depending on the decisions that the model is required to support
Time Bucket	The level of time precision that is required to support the process. It does not have to be the same as the S&OP cycle. For example, a model can have a time bucket of 1 week, with results aggregated to the monthly level for reporting.
Objective	A mathematical expression representing the goals that a planner wants to achieve. This could be minimizing overall costs, or maximizing total revenue, or margin.
Aggregation and Classification	The precision at which products, capacity, and customers are to be represented in the model.
Parameters	Examples include costs, capacities, and margins. The costs might include packaging costs, transport costs, and manufacturing costs.
Constraints	These are restrictions that place limitations on how the supply chain goal can be achieved. There could be constraints on distribution, packaging, and manufacturing. These typically include capacity, transport, lot size or campaign restrictions, available warehouse capacity and others.

Identifying Business Parameters

Raw Material Restrictions

- Identify the major raw materials and list their constraints.

- Determine the alternative sources for supply and the lead times.

- Is there a hold time before materials can be used for production?

- Does material have to be ordered in multiples of quantities such as, whole rail car loads?

Representing Capacity

How should manufacturing capacity be represented, overall throughput, feed capacity, or specific equipment constraints on furnaces, docks, and others? Questions like, "Can additional capacity be added at a higher cost?", or "Do we need to limit number of changeovers?", need to be clarified.

What determines the amount of capacity consumed? Is it a function of product mix, operation mode or production rate? Is production rate time dependent (ramp up / ramp down)? Are there other factors which affect how capacity is consumed?

On average, what percent of capacity is lost due to changeovers? What is the frequency of changeovers? As changeovers are not modeled explicitly inside planning models, what approximation strategies would be appropriate to allow for lost capacity due to changeovers? One possibility is to assume a certain number of changeovers per time period.

What types of service factor and reliability issues are present? What are some typical causes of un-planned downtime? Is a historic value for downtime meaningful? Is it better to allow some down time to compensate for unplanned outages, or is it better to assume a lower production rate?

What types of calendar functionality are required? Is it possible to run parts of the process in an overtime mode (e.g. a production line that runs 5 days for 2 shifts but could run at other times at a premium cost)? Are there shutdowns due to holidays – are they location / unit specific or system wide? Are there manpower restrictions on capacity?

Production Representation

Are there multiple ways of making the same product on units or production lines? What types of things characterize a production mode (e.g. feedstock, unit severity, etc)? How many operating modes need to be represented – and what things are functions of the operating mode (e.g. yield, production rate, capacity consumption, cost, feed used, etc.)

Do factors such as operating mode, feed type / quality, or production unit determine production yields? How do yields vary with time, feed quality, and other factors?

Are there minimum or maximum production quantities or run lengths? Why do these constraints exist?

How many stages of production are there in a process or a plant? How different stages of production are *linked* (intermediate inventory). Is there a time lag that needs to be modeled between production stages? For example, quality control may require minimum time between stages.

Is blending required before the product is packaged? (Fixed recipe blending / specification blending)?

Is there a make – buy decision that needs to be made? What should the basis for making this decision be? What factors should be considered in determining tradeoffs of making early and storing vs. buying?

Does a recipe create multiple products, co-products or by-products? Do the by-products have an inventory constraint or production constraint? Are there products we must make to fulfill contractual requirements?

Inventory

List all points of inventory that need to be included; raw materials, intermediate, finished, in transit, other.

List all locations where inventory is held and types of inventory held at each location. Is there any consigned inventory?

What limits maximum inventory that can be held – e.g. physical constraints. Can additional inventory capacity (external warehouses, rail cars, etc.) be acquired, presumably at higher costs? Will it cause problems for inventory buildups for planned shutdowns?

How is safety stock (minimum inventory) or target inventory to be modeled? Is the minimum inventory level a soft minimum that can be violated with a penalty? Is safety stock represented as a volume (or weight minimum) or thought of in terms of days of supply? Is safety stock seasonal or time dependent?

Do we need to segregate inventory based on production information such as production unit, feed stock or other criterion (e.g. required when certain customers will only accept product with specific attributes or manufacturing characteristics).

Are there any aggregate inventory constraints like total warehouse space?

What are the issues associated with obtaining starting inventory or inventory 'snap shots' required in the model. Is it based on physical inventory or on computed values? How accurate are the values? How should in-transit inventory be accounted for? Is there data on when in-transit inventory will reach destination?

Transportation

What factors determine valid ship-to and ship-from combinations?

Which modes can be used between each ship-to and ship-from location combination? What criteria is used to select transportation modes (e.g. cost)?

What other types of transportation constraints need to be modeled? Possibilities include dock capacity, loading – unloading capacity, total capacity by transportation mode, and downtimes for shipping and receiving.

Is there a need to model integer shipments? This may involve requirements around full truck loads.

Demand Representation

What type of demand information will be available for planning? Will product by location by time period be sufficient or is more detail required?

Is there a concept of demand classes or tiers for pricing, priority or other reasons?

Can product substitution occur? For instance, can we supply higher quality grade for lower quality demand? Describe the rules around product substitutions.

Do we need to model demand by customer? If pricing is customer dependent, we may want to decide which customers to supply.

Does all demand have to be satisfied? What would be the criteria for demand violation? Can demand be price driven and only supplied if profitable?

Do we need to model specific orders with the demands vs. aggregate or net demand forecast? If yes – explain why?

Other Constraints

Are there any other types of constraints other than capacity, inventory, and transportation that need to be considered, such as labor? If yes describe how these other resources should be allocated when constrained.

Do we need to model product and feedstock exchange agreements? What is the contractual basis of such agreements? Is there a need to track and manage agreement imbalances?

Are there location / product differentials that need to be considered?

Economic Representations

List all costs that need to be considered such as raw material, production, transportation, inventory carrying, energy, labor and overtime, product exchanges, etc.

What economics need to be considered in the make/buy decisions?

What should the optimizer's objective function be, minimize costs, maximize revenue or profit. Is meaningful revenue / price data available?

Example of a Planning Model for a Multi Site Manufacturing Company

A complete explanation of Linear Programming and supply chain modeling is out of scope of this book. This section illustrates some of the key decision variables, parameters, and constraints that are normally included when constructing a model for process manufacturers like a chemical company.

Decision Variables

Variable Type	Explanation
Ending Inventory	The level of ending inventory at the end of each time bucket. A separate variable is defined for each combination of raw, intermediate and finished product, stocking location, and planning time period.
Purchase	The amount of raw material purchased at each location in each planning time period.
Production	The amount of each finished product and intermediate that is produced on a manufacturing facility in each planning time period.
Filled Orders	The amount of open orders of each finished product that we plan to fill in each planning period.
Filled Forecast	The amount of forecast of a product at a location that we intend to supply in each planning period.
Difference from target inventory	The difference between the ending inventory and the target inventory for each time period and for each finished, intermediate, and raw material for which we have defined a target.
Internal material transfers	The amount of each finished and intermediate material shipped between any two locations, in each planning period.

Horizon and Precision

Time Horizon	18 Months
Time Bucket	Month

Objective

Objective	Maximize (Total sales revenue – manufacturing costs – storage costs – transport costs)

Aggregation and Classification

Products	Aggregated to a grade level. Each family consists of up to 3 or 4 SKU's. Bill of Materials between the products in a grade only varies by package type. *In the rest of the discussion, product, family, and grade will be used interchangeably.*
Customers	Top 10 customers with the remaining customers grouped into one representative customer

Parameters

Parameter Type	Explanation
Open Orders and Month-to-Date Shipments	These are used to net the forecast. The open orders are filled with higher priority than the forecast.
Starting Inventory	The amount of each grade that is available at each location at the beginning of the first planning bucket.
Inventory targets	The desired amount of ending inventory for each grade and location. This target is normally used to buffer against demand and supply variability within the planning bucket.
Production rates	The rate for each allowable combination of production facility and grade (finished or intermediate).
Capacity	Capacity is usually represented as the hours of machine time available for each facility.

Parameter Type	Explanation
Transport times	When transferring material from one location to another within the model, the transport times are used to estimate the period in which inventory depletes from a location, and the period in which it is made available at the destination.
Costs	Costs include production costs, inventory holding costs, raw material procurement and material costs, and transport costs.
Prices	These are used to calculate the planned revenue.
Planning Bill of Materials	This is used to estimate the production and procurement of intermediate and raw materials.
Product to Family mapping	Normally, the calculations are done at the individual grade level within the model. However, for reporting, it is convenient to aggregate the results by one or more families.

Constraints

Inventory Balance Equations

These equations are used to ensure that there is material balance for each combination of material, time period, and location. Each equation represents the sum of all inputs and outputs to the inventory of a product at a location in a given planning bucket. If the sum of all inputs and outputs is positive, this means that inventory is created and it is transferred to the next planning bucket as the starting inventory. The sum of the inputs (including the starting inventory) and outputs cannot of course be negative.

The inputs to a finished material inventory at a location consist of the starting inventory, any production at the location, and transfers from other locations. Outputs consist of any material used to fill orders, material used to fill forecasts, material transferred to another location, and the amount of material kept for the next planning period.

For intermediate and raw materials, the amount of purchases is an additional input. Material can also be depleted if it is used to support production of another material. Actual depletions are defined by the bill of material.

Capacity Balance Equations

The amount of production that can be made is limited by the available capacity. Each capacity balance equation limits the total production on a facility in each planning time bucket. The linear program is used to allocate the facility's available time between competing production requirements in the most profitable manner.

Normally, the capacity is represented as the number of hours of production time available in a month. Production of a material consumes the available time and total time used to produce all materials cannot exceed the available time on the machine.

Bookkeeping Equations

In a comprehensive supply /demand balancing model, there are usually a number of constraints that are used to calculate the net forecast, the difference between actual inventory and the targets, and spare capacity. Bookkeeping constraints may include equations to calculate the net forecast for the rest of the month, the amount by which the inventory is above or below the target, and so on.

Model Validation and Calibration

The model needs to be intuitively plausible before it can be relied on for decisions affecting the future. Normally this is done by comparing the results of the model with actual performance for an identified period in the past.

The validation of the model is usually done in two stages:

1. The first stage is to ensure that the physical production and movement of material is similar to what was experienced.

2. The second stage is to ensure that the model reflects the cost and revenue flow.

The procedures for model validation are described below. Each procedure is described in terms of the variables that should be controlled, the results that should be checked, and the areas which should be looked at if there are significant discrepancies.

Physical Flow of Material

Procedure for Validating Production	
Control Variables	Make sure that shutdowns are reflected Fix the demand to the amount that actually shipped Constrain the production to occur only on the facilities that it occurred during the period being tested
Look for	No demand shortages Capacity utilization that is similar to what was experienced
In Case of Discrepancies	Check production rates or production by day Check for unscheduled downtimes on facilities Check that transport routes are adequately defined from production sources to demand locations
Procedure for Validating Distribution	
Control Variables	Make sure that shutdowns are reflected Fix the demand to the amount that actually shipped Constrain the production to occur only on the facilities that it occurred during the period being tested Only allow shipment channels that have been used in the period being tested

Look for	No demand shortages
	Capacity utilization that is similar to what was experienced
	Shipment quantities that are the same as those experienced during the test period
In Case of Discrepancies	Check for missing transport routes
	Check locations where a product is not allowed to be stored in the model
	Check lead times

Costs and Revenue

Procedure for Checking Costs	
Control Variables	Relax the production restrictions so that these do not affect the results
	Relax the transport restrictions to all possible modes
	Fix the demand to the amount that actually shipped
	Constrain the production to occur only on the facilities that it occurred during the period being tested
	Only allow shipment channels that have been used in the period being tested
Look for	Total costs to be lower than all previous scenarios
	No inventory buildup in products that are not sold
	Production costs to be similar to those experienced in the past
	Transport costs to be similar to those experienced in the past

In Case of Discrepancies	Check minimum and maximum values on target inventory
	Check manufacturing costs plus transport costs which are higher than selling prices
	Check point to point transport costs
	Check rates on facilities
	Check variable manufacturing costs

Verify System Behavior

To verify system behavior, you need to define scenarios for the model. Each scenario should be defined together with the expected results. The model results should then be analyzed to make sure that the behavior is consistent. An example scenario is shown below

Scenario: Increase variable costs	
Changes Expected	Increase production costs on machine X by 200%
	Demand for products a, b, d should move to machine Y
	Demand for customer x and y will not be met

Other scenarios that should be validated include:

- Planned shutdown

- A significant increase in demand

- A significant reduction in demand

- Price fluctuations over time

Metrics and Performance Measurement

You Cannot Improve What You Can't Measure

To sustain a quality supply chain process, it is necessary to measure the quality of the monthly plan and how well the execution adheres to the plan. The monthly plan reflects the direction in which the business is headed. This plan must be compared with the annual budgets to ensure compliance with the organization's goals. It also provides feedback on overall inventory levels, utilizations, and demand trends. Metrics that use aggregated monthly data are normally presented at the Sales and Operations Planning (S&OP) meeting.

During the month, there are daily fluctuations that occur. These reflect changes in capacity or demand and most should not require re-planning. However, when the cumulative effect of the daily fluctuations reaches a critical point, the plan should be recreated or modified.

Performance monitoring and management is not all about creating charts and displays. It starts with identifying undesirable *consequences* for the business or the customer. These then lead to a systematic analysis of the reasons or *concerns* that result in the consequences.

The status of consequences against goals and overall trends are best measured periodically. These measurements should lead directly to actions that improve the planning process. To enable a business to respond quickly, the period metrics need to be supported with daily monitoring which is focused on identifying perturbations or *causes* that could lead to disruptions. While the monthly metrics provide guidance on how to modify the planning process and the S&OP plan, monitoring the daily fluctuations allows a business to detect signals early and respond accordingly. The two types of measurements are complementary, and both are needed in an effective supply chain process.

Most everyone can agree that measuring a process is a cornerstone for improvement. But measurement alone is of little use. If the measurement is out of line, specific actions need to be taken to bring the process back in line. For this reason, metrics need to be constructed so that they lead to targeted improvement. As the business evolves over time, the metrics used will change. Different metrics will be used at different times depending on the improvement area which is being targeted.

Causes, Concerns and Consequences

To develop metrics for the supply chain, we must first identify the *concerns*. Typically these fall into four categories;

Concerns	Examples
Financial Performance	1. Working capital too high 2. Supply chain costs are tracking above budget
Delivery Performance	1. Product is not available for a customer to whom we had previously promised a date using the ATP process 2. Inventory levels are too low to support normal demand variability
Supply Performance	1. Proportion of off-quality material is too high 2. Raw material is not available to run production 3. Machine is down because of an unplanned shutdown
Environment and External Factors	1. Transport shortage 2. Weather

A concern is the result of one or more *causes* and represents an issue that needs to be addressed. If it is not addressed then undesirable *consequences* will follow. A key role of performance measurement is to identify imbalances before they develop into a concern. Hence proactive performance monitoring should concentrate primarily on causes.

One concern can have many consequences. Consequences do not always have the same impact on the business, even in similar situations. For example, in a situation where the market is soft, we might want to protect ALL customers. On the other hand, if the market is tight, we may want to protect only key customers. Our response is driven both by internal supply chain concerns as well as by external factors.

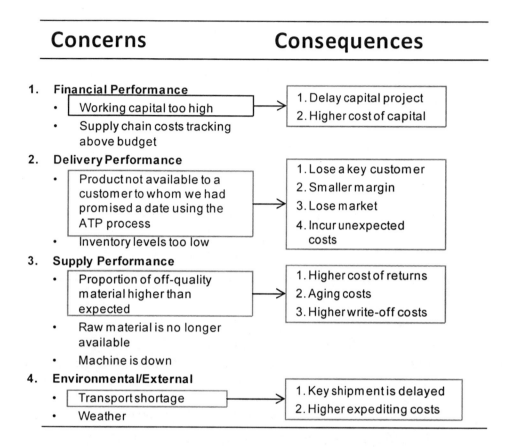

Concerns	Consequences
1. Financial Performance • Working capital too high • Supply chain costs tracking above budget	1. Delay capital project 2. Higher cost of capital
2. Delivery Performance • Product not available to a customer to whom we had promised a date using the ATP process • Inventory levels too low	1. Lose a key customer 2. Smaller margin 3. Lose market 4. Incur unexpected costs
3. Supply Performance • Proportion of off-quality material higher than expected • Raw material is no longer available • Machine is down	1. Higher cost of returns 2. Aging costs 3. Higher write-off costs
4. Environmental/External • Transport shortage • Weather	1. Key shipment is delayed 2. Higher expediting costs

Because the impact of a concern is not always the same on the business, the planner is the best person to decide what mitigating action to initiate.

A concern is inevitably caused by supply chain imbalances. For example, the diagram below illustrates some of the potential causes for the concern that "*product will not be available to ship on the promised date*".

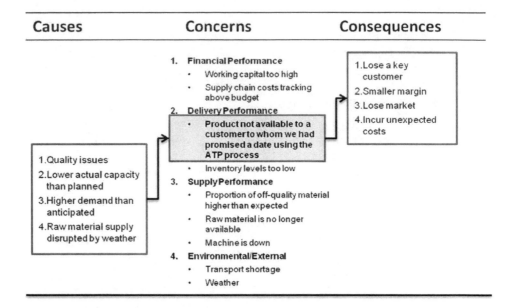

Causes	Concerns	Consequences

1. **Financial Performance**
   - Working capital too high
   - Supply chain costs tracking above budget
2. **Delivery Performance**
   - **Product not available to a customer to whom we had promised a date using the ATP process**
   - Inventory levels too low
3. **Supply Performance**
   - Proportion of off-quality material higher than expected
   - Raw material is no longer available
   - Machine is down
4. **Environmental/External**
   - Transport shortage
   - Weather

Causes:
1. Quality issues
2. Lower actual capacity than planned
3. Higher demand than anticipated
4. Raw material supply disrupted by weather

Consequences:
1. Lose a key customer
2. Smaller margin
3. Lose market
4. Incur unexpected costs

The Bowtie Diagram

The *bowtie* diagram for each concern illustrates the relationships between causes, concerns, and consequences. For example, let's take the case where a previously committed order cannot ship because of a lack of inventory. The promise date to the customer was provided by the ATP system, but the CSR detects that there is insufficient inventory available to ship this order.

If the product does not ship on time, there could be consequences. These could be:

- Customer may cancel this order and we lose the associated margin.

- We could lose a key customer because the missed order degrades the relationship.

- The order may be for a non-key and low margin customer which has very little impact.

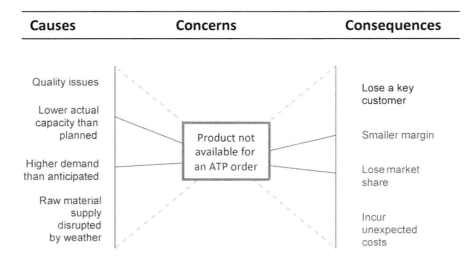

Causes	Concerns	Consequences

Quality issues

Lower actual capacity than planned

Higher demand than anticipated

Raw material supply disrupted by weather

Product not available for an ATP order

Lose a key customer

Smaller margin

Lose market share

Incur unexpected costs

There should be a well understood and well defined process to mitigate the effects of any concern. Normally this response is stored in a commonly accessible place. Mitigating actions could include:

- Buy material from a competitor and deliver on time

- Renegotiate the delivery date

- Expedite transport

These are represented on the diagram as *blockers* to interrupt the path to consequences. In effect they are the crisis management rules that a company uses to mitigate the effect of the concerns.

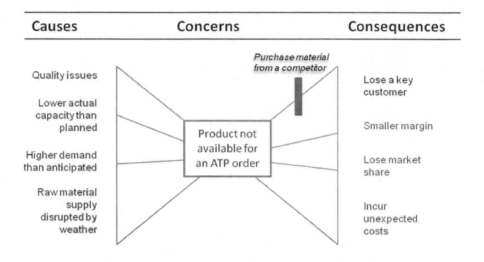

Similarly, re-planning tries to stop a concern from materializing.

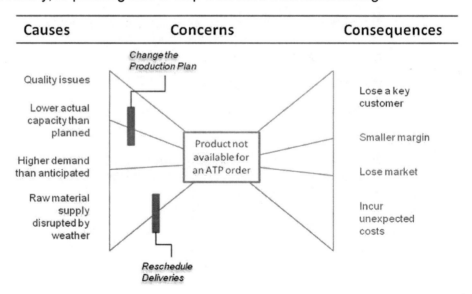

A full set of re-planning barriers may include:

- Change the production plan

- Move production to contract facilities

- Improve quality checking

- Reschedule delivery dates

- Use express service for raw materials

- Improve the S&OP process to better coordinate the supply and demand

Early warning indicators are designed to detect imbalances, and are normally related to a *cause*. While the purpose of the re-planning barriers is to protect against a cause becoming a concern, early warning indicators are used to determine when a cause is likely to occur.

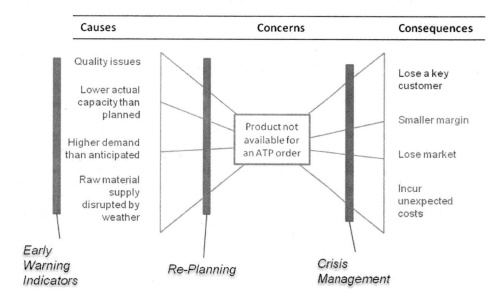

Hence for each of the causes, a suitable measurement should be identified as an early warning indication. Monthly measurements are useful for highlighting systemic issues, but cannot be used to respond to daily issues.

In a comprehensive performance management implementation, both early warning indicators and monthly metrics are required.

For the example above, suitable metrics are:

Cause	Early Warning	Monthly Measurement
Lower Actual Capacity	Percent uptime for this month, tracked each day, versus expected	Actual production divided by scheduled production
Quality Issues	Percentage of production rejected in quality checks versus normal levels	Monthly yield by production unit versus the plan
Higher Demand than Planned	Open order volume versus normal for this time of the month	Total shipments divided by the total forecast
Product Supplied to Non-promised Customers	Higher than normal "next-day" shipments.	Number of shipments delayed to key customers
Raw Material Shortage	Raw material inventory + (on-order) – (requirements in the next X days)	Raw material days supply versus target

Implementation

Implementation normally follows the following process.

1. Identify and document the concerns of the business and the potential consequences. This is normally done through interviews with planners and decision makers, and reconciling these with the business goals and targets

2. List potential causes and corrective action. Identify the cause/concern matrix through detailed knowledge of the business and applying supply chain best practices.

3. Identify data needed to support early warning indicators. The data requirements need to be meshed with what data is available.

4. Audit and refine the metrics

Monitoring and Early Warning

Early warning indicators raise a flag when the underlying process may be out of control. This system supports the business manager or analyst by monitoring the "health" of the current sales and operations plan. The business manager/supply-chain manager must be able to detect at a glance if the current plan needs to be revised or if other corrective action needs to be initiated. The specific elements of the supply chain activity are monitored on a daily basis. These measurements will be charted much like a "process control chart".

The following table provides one example of how a selection of metrics can be used to measure the supply chain process.

Cause	Example Measurements
Unusual Demand	• Number of open orders that have not been shipped • Month to date orders vs. forecast • Total volume on orders
Unusual Receivables	• Total value of receivables • Weighted dollar days (Sum of the value of each invoice * days since it was issued / Total value of all invoices) • Shipped and not invoiced orders

Cause	Example Measurements
Logistics Issues	• Month to date expediting costs • Number of shipments expedited • Unavailability of trucks/rail cars (on-hand + estimated arrivals – requirements)
Purchasing Issues	• Availability of raw materials (Days of Supply). Raw material volume / average usage – for critical raw materials. This should be measured both in terms of value as well as units. • Quality of raw materials
Manufacturing Issues	• Schedule reliability • Schedule adherence – cumulative scheduled production versus cumulative completed production • Total daily production
Process Reliability	• Yield – volume of scrap and second quality • Number of lots tested
Physical Distribution	• Number of empty railcars at the site • Number of trucks shipped

In summary, an early warning measurement:

1. Tracks a cause with respect to an acceptable or normal change

2. Provides a notification process that is invoked if the measurement is out of the normal range

3. Provides the ability to track the measurement over time.

Monthly Measurements

The intent of the monthly measurements is to:

• Detect systematic changes to the process (should this be systemic?)

- Verify that the plans support annual goals and the budget
- Verify that the supply chain performance is consistent with the plans

Periodic measurements are useful because they reduce the day to day variability and provide a more stable measure of performance. However, they always need to be supported with more detailed daily monitoring to increase response.

Useful monthly metrics have two characteristics:

1. The metrics should be cross functional or presented simultaneously with other metrics. For example, it is better to monitor how well the inventory supports the forecast than to measure forecast accuracy and inventory volumes independently.

2. The measurement should be presented within context. It should show the value with respect to the desired range or target, and should also indicate how the measurement has changed.

Sustaining Supply Chain Planning Improvements

In the preceding chapters we have described how to implement a tactical supply chain planning process in small incremental steps. Over the years, we have found that an incremental process like this is much more successful than a "big-bang" approach.

Indeed, supply chain improvement involves a series of projects separated by periods of institutionalization. Unfortunately, during these periods, there are many opportunities to regress to the "old ways of doing things." In our experience, a successful project is *necessary but not sufficient* for sustainable supply chain improvement.

Software vendors have encouraged companies to implement supply chain applications as isolated projects that are started and finished. Such applications serve the purpose of consultants and software companies because they can sell specific products and services. Companies also like this approach because they measure progress towards a goal in a limited time interval. In our experience, this approach is risky and improvements are not sustained, because as soon as the project is completed, old practices tend to creep back.

Why Do Companies Regress?

Reason #1: The software doesn't do what I need it to do.

Because modern supply chain software is flexible, it can be configured to do practically anything. But even though the initial implementation addresses a company's needs, over time business conditions change. If the software does not adapt to the changes, it becomes too cumbersome. People invent alternatives. In today's environment, creating these alternatives is relatively easy with desktop tools like Excel and Access. Although these homegrown systems may appear to help at first, they often end up as isolated applications that need a lot of care and feeding. As a result, data becomes decentralized, and the old inefficiencies creep back in.

Reason #2: The users move on.

Supply chain planning applications are notoriously complex because many of these applications were developed with heavy involvement from the initial users. While such involvement ensured their success, it also meant that certain ways of doing things - unique to the initial set of users - were introduced as well. In addition, large companies often do a poor job of preparing and training replacements for professional jobs like planning. Frequently the employee new to this job has a limited time to acquire the skills and absorb the intricacies of the tools that need to be managed. The net result is that the application is used less frequently and gradually is replaced by spreadsheets or other applications that may be simpler but less effective.

Reason #3: The planning is too successful.

Supply chain improvements usually occur in response to specific business needs and are articulated in terms of a business crisis like "too much inventory," "missed shipments," etc. Since many of these issues are mitigated with proper supply chain planning, it is difficult to quantify the benefit of something that eliminates problems before they occur. Over time, planning is perceived as no longer an issue and the business process is streamlined to eliminate much of the planning function.

When Do Companies Sustain Improvements?

In our experience, the companies that sustain improvements have three things in common:

- **They consider supply chain planning and execution to be a key competency,** and because of this, they recognize that ongoing efforts must be made to maintain their advantage in supply chain operations. Often, these companies have a distinct supply chain organization with the same clout as the manufacturing, logistics, and sales organizations.

- **Supply Chain management is viewed as a professional activity.** Scheduling, for example, is not regarded as a clerical activity; instead, it is recognized as a job that requires proper training and skills. These companies recognize that schedulers and planners frequently make decisions that alter working capital by millions of dollars. Decisions of this magnitude that affect other assets in a company usually require an extensive review process.

- Within an overall Information Systems (IS) strategy, **these companies are constantly looking for improved technology** to make the work processes more effective. As a result, they can respond to business crises rapidly, and if necessary, develop tools that can be institutionalized and absorbed over time.

  Because these companies also recognize that it is important to seize the initiative when there is a business focus on a supply chain issue, they then create step-change improvements. For example, a supply crisis may lead to improved scheduling; an inventory write-down may lead to improved testing procedures, and so on.

- **Software is viewed as a tool that needs to be adapted to their process**. Many companies attempt to avoid the hard work required to change by implementing software that purports to provide "best practices". This approach tries to use software to enforce compliance to the processes embedded in the software system. Our experience is that this is not successful because planners tend to gravitate to spreadsheets and other aids when the process embedded in the software system does not allow them to make good decisions easily. The net result is that a number of parallel processes are developed and the software system becomes increasingly irrelevant.

The more successful companies understand that software tools and systems must elicit the commitment of the users. They need to be adapted to changing circumstances so that they can continue to support the S&OP process effectively.

What Can Companies Do?

- Provide ongoing education and training to those functions that can impact the supply chain by their decisions. For example, supply chain training in half-day sessions for functions like sales or manufacturing can be very effective.

- Encourage the professionals who manage the supply chain to upgrade and improve their skills. Companies typically allow training but do not require it.

- Make sure that the supply chain decisions are transparent to allow broad access to the supply chain data. Transparency is the first step to fostering internal collaboration.

- Develop a structure and a budget that allows the supply chain to rapidly respond to business crises with improved tools.

- Recognize achievements and internally publicize specific successes.

Breinigsville, PA USA
18 December 2009

229462BV00003B/1/P